W9-AZD-666

Animals of the
Polar Regions

LEVEL READER

READING LEVEL
2
GRADES 1 TO 3

The most southern land on Earth is a huge continent called Antarctica. It is covered with ice about 6,500 feet thick. The temperature here sometimes drops to −125° F. In winter, the ocean around Antarctica forms layers of pack ice. Many animals make their home on this ice and along the coasts.

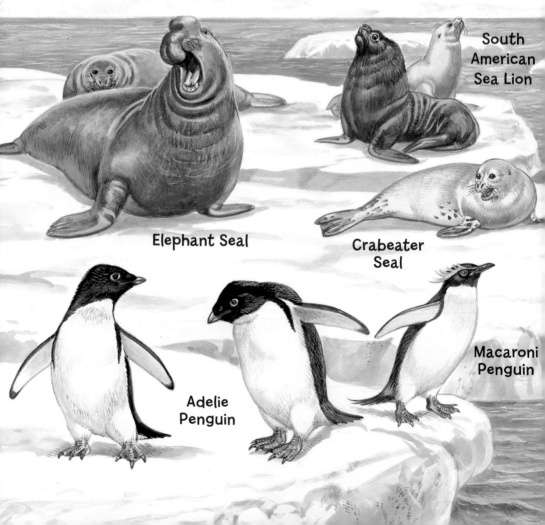

South American Sea Lion

Elephant Seal

Crabeater Seal

Adelie Penguin

Macaroni Penguin

Wandering Albatross

King Penguin

Emperor Penguin

Ross Seal

Weddell Seal

Leopard Seal

Emperor Penguin

There are many kinds of penguins that live on or near Antarctica. The largest is the emperor. It stands up to four feet tall. Like all penguins, the emperor has short wings, but cannot fly. It uses its wings to swim underwater.

While the females hunt during the winter, the males take care of the eggs.

Adelie Penguin

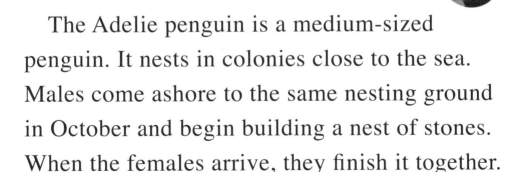

The Adelie penguin is a medium-sized penguin. It nests in colonies close to the sea. Males come ashore to the same nesting ground in October and begin building a nest of stones. When the females arrive, they finish it together.

King Penguin

The king penguin is a big penguin that also nests in huge colonies. The female lays an egg at the beginning of spring, and parents take turns *incubating* it (keeping it warm) for two months. After the chicks hatch, they huddle together to keep warm.

Chinstrap Penguin

These small penguins have bands of black feathers under their chins—like chinstraps. Their star-shaped pupils *contract* (get smaller) to protect their eyes from sun glare on the ice. Then they *dilate* (grow larger) in the dark.

Rockhopper Penguin

A rockhopper penguin has bright yellow feathers on its head. It nests on sheer cliffs high above the sea. Its strong curved claws help it climb and hop from rock to rock.

African Penguin

Not all penguins live in the far polar regions. African penguins live off the southern coast of Africa. They raise their chicks on land.

Galapagos Penguin

The Galapagos penguin, one of the world's smallest penguins, lives near the Equator. Why are these penguins here? Because many years ago, penguins swam in a cold current running up the coast of South America from the polar region. They landed on the Galapagos Islands.

Leopard Seal

Penguins of the Antarctic have one main predator—the leopard seal. The leopard seal moves fast with its long, bendable body. It can grow to 10 feet long and weigh 1000 pounds. The leopard seal can open its mouth very wide. This allows the seal to swallow huge mouthfuls!

Antarctic Seals

There are many seals in the Antarctic. As the sea freezes over, some seals *migrate* (move from one area to another). Others do not. They use their sharp teeth to open holes in the ice to surface and breathe.

Crabeater seals live in small groups, fishing, sunbathing, or just drifting on ice. You might think they eat crabs, but they actually feed mainly on krill—tiny shrimplike animals.

Ross seals live in the ocean, hanging out around pack ice and icebergs. Their pups are born on drifting ice sheets, safe from enemies.

Weddell seals live the farthest south inside the Antarctic Circle.

Ross Seal

Crabeater Seal

Weddell Seal

Elephant Seal

There are elephant seals in both the Antarctic and Arctic regions. These seals are large. Males weigh up to 8,000 pounds. They have small teeth, yet they eat squid, fish, and even sharks.

South American Sea Lion

This sea lion is covered with thick fur, and males have manes. Unlike seals, the sea lion has true ears and can turn its rear flippers forward to move faster. Their rear flippers have small claws used for scratching and grooming.

The Arctic Region

The North Pole is in the middle of the Arctic Ocean. A big area around the Pole is covered with floating ice that forms an icecap. In summer, ice thaws on the land areas and mosses, grasses, and low bushes grow. This is called the *tundra*.

Narwhal

Polar Bear

Pomarine Jaeger

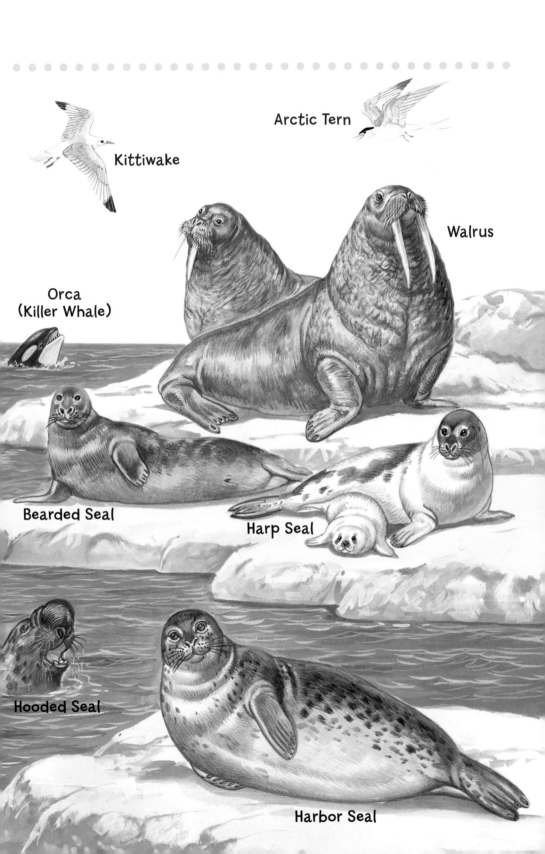

Kittiwake

Arctic Tern

Walrus

Orca
(Killer Whale)

Bearded Seal

Harp Seal

Hooded Seal

Harbor Seal

Polar Bear

The polar bear is the largest land *carnivorous* (flesh-eating) mammal. In winter, an adult male can weigh 2,200 pounds. This bear travels on pack ice and swims between ice sheets. Its white fur is thick and *water-repellant* (doesn't soak up water). Thick layers of fat protect it from the biting cold and keep it afloat.

Polar bears feed on seals, fish, and small mammals. When the ocean throws dead fish onto the beach, polar bears have a feast!

As winter starts, a female digs out a small den in the snow, close to the sea. She gives birth to one or two cubs. The mother keeps them warm with her breath.

Walrus

Male walruses can weigh more than 3,500 pounds when their blubber is thickest. Their brownish skin is wrinkled and about an inch thick. They live in herds of about a hundred. Their main predator is the orca (killer whale).

The walrus's tusks are actually two upper teeth that never stop growing.

Walruses eat shellfish, worms, starfish, and sea urchins from the ocean floor. They can stay underwater for five to ten minutes at a time.

Females give birth to a pup weighing about a hundred pounds. The newborn pup can swim. It follows its mother into the water soon after birth. The mother protects her pup from predators and cares for it for a year.

Harbor Seal

The harbor seal is clumsy on land—crawling like a caterpillar. But this seal is an expert in the water. Big eyes help it spot fish even in poor light. It can stay underwater up to forty-five minutes!

Harbor seals can eat eleven pounds of fish a day. They love fish from the ocean floor, but also eat crabs, squid, and shellfish. Sometimes harbor seals break into fishermen's nets for a quick meal.

Arctic Seals

The most common seals of the northern polar region are the gray seal, harp seal, ringed seal, and hooded seal. They live in the open ocean and gather on drifting ice to rest and give birth.

Gray Seal

Hooded Seal

Ringed Seal

Harp Seal

Arctic Fox

This beautiful fox has thick layers of fat and fur that keep it warm in the cold Arctic. In winter, its fur is white, so it blends in with the snow. In summer, its coat can be gray or brown.

The Arctic fox eats mostly lemmings. It also likes plants, berries, fruits and bird eggs.

Lemming

The lemming is a small rodent with a short tail. It is *nocturnal* (active at night) and digs burrows to hide from predators.

Arctic Hare

The Arctic hare stays snowy white all year long. Its paws are covered with thick fur, which helps it run faster over soft snow.